Visions on Alligator Alley

visions on alligator alley

ekphrastic story in verse by Laura McDermott

Published by Lominy Books
Davie, Florida
lominybooks.com

First Edition, 2015
Copyright © 2015 Laura McDermott

The views expressed in this book are those of the author and artists, and do not necessarily reflect those of the publisher.

All rights reserved. All images copyright the artists. This book, or parts thereof, may not be reproduced in any form without permission from the publisher, the author, the artists and their legal representatives. The scanning, uploading, and distribution of this book via the Internet or via any other means without the permission of the publisher is illegal and punishable by law. Please purchase only authorized editions, and do not participate in or encourage piracy of copyrighted materials. Your support of the author's and artists' rights is appreciated.

"Mechanics," "A Childhood Glossary of Automechanics," "Glossary of a First Love," "Glossary of a Heartbreak," and "Glossary of the Dating Bluebook" first appeared in *Poets & Artists*, August 1, 2013
"Ampersand" first appeared in *Eight Cent Journal: A Modern Anthology of Miami Poets*, April 9, 2011
"Rolling Back the Odometer" first appeared in *One Cent Journal: A Modern Anthology of Miami Poets*, February 6, 2009
"Visions on Alligator Alley" received Third Honorable Mention in the 2013 Poetry Society of Virginia's Adult Contest
"Rebirth" has been performed by Jenny Larsson for live audiences in South Florida.
"When the Mechanics Go Home" and "Roses" appear in the 2015 Girls' Club Foundation catalog, "The Moment. The Backdrop. The Persona."

All artwork featured in this book was on display in the Girls' Club Ft. Lauderdale exhibit "The Moment. The Backdrop. The Persona." November 7, 2014 — September 26, 2015.

Cover Photo: Rosemary Laing, "one dozen unnatural disasters in the Australian landscape #2," 2003, C Type Photograph, 48⅗ x 86½" © Rosemary Laing, Courtesy Galerie Lelong, New York.

Book Design: Charlotte Howard, CKH Design
The text is set in Candara, a humanist sans-serif typeface designed by Gary Munch and released in 2006. The titles are set in DIN Alternate, a sans-serif signage face released by Stempel in 1923 and updated in 1995 by Albert-Jan Pool.

ISBN: 978-0-9910821-9-3

Printed in the United States of America.

In the college dormitory, many years ago, he mentioned his interest in poetry, and then shared a poem about me while I thumbed through a muscle car magazine. I set out to learn as much as I could about the art, and he read some of my poems. Out of respect for my work, instead of giving criticism, he encouraged me to write more.

He applauded my accomplishments and accolades, continuously reminding me to make time for poetry—to never lose focus. As I received tenure, worked for non-profits and then started my own non-profit, he reminded me to take time for myself in order to cultivate my art.

For this, I dedicate this book to you, Walter, my husband and biggest cheerleader. You never allowed me to lose my relationship with poetry despite the clutter of everyday life. Thank you.

To our daughter, Jordan, and to the little one joining us in December: you are the best poems your Daddy and I have ever collaborated on.

ekphrastic (ek-FRAS-tick)

From the Greek *ekphrasis* (ECK-fray-sis or ek-FRAS-iss) meaning "description."

A vivid description of a scene or, more commonly, a work of art. Through the imaginative act of narrating and reflecting on the "action" of a painting or sculpture, the poet may amplify and expand its meaning.
Notable example: "Ode on a Grecian Urn" by John Keats.

— Poetry Foundation

Foreword

Although a picture is worth a thousand words, finding a path to understanding works of visual art via language is a rich occupation. Like identifying a sound that correlates to a color, or discovering the exact dance movement that corresponds to a specific musical phrase, addressing a picture with words can open up understanding, intensify it.

When we invited Laura McDermott to be Girls' Club's 2014-15 Writer-in-Residence, the exhibition we were planning seemed to suit a writer perfectly. "The Moment. The Backdrop. The Persona." assembles works by thirty-eight artists from the collection of Francie Bishop Good and David Horvitz, each interpreting narrative in varying ways. The exhibition, curated by Sarah Michelle Rupert and myself, responds to the recent resurgence of narrative in contemporary art.

The poems in this book do not merely translate the visual into the verbal. Each one absorbs the multivalent experience of a painting, drawing, print, photo or video work, and then effects some sympathetic conversion, a transposition of that experience into an independent work of art. In 1957 Marcel Duchamp described the "art coefficient," an arithmetical relation between "the unexpressed but intended and the unintentionally expressed." He factored the necessary role played by the spectator in the existence of a work of art, assuring us that the creative act is not performed by the artist alone. McDermott activates that art coefficient in this book.

By linking her poems into one work, *Visions on Alligator Alley* is a modest epic of sorts. Each of McDermott's observations functions as a chapter, an episode, a mini-moment of whopping clarity or a slow unfolding of recognition. Her poems frame powerful moments and compress their meaning into lines on the printed page. She enters and inhabits the frontiers constructed by the artists' works, and she tunes her ear to the human voice. The *ekphrasis,* begun as an ancient Greek rhetorical exercise, takes a detour into South Florida. Palm fronds and engine compartments, cell phones and bar counters, Coppertone tans and memories of parked cars, love, marriage, divorce, combustion, pistons, more cars, a Mustang, a Mercedes, a Falcon, an American vernacular.

— Michelle Weinberg, Creative Director, Girls' Club[†]
July 2015

[†] Established in 2006, Girls' Club is an alternative exhibition space in downtown Fort Lauderdale that presents annual thematic exhibitions of contemporary art by women from the collection of Francie Bishop Good and David Horvitz. The mission of Girls' Club is to educate the public, nurture the careers of female artists, and to serve as a resource for art students and scholars, curators, and practicing artists. www.girlsclubcollection.org

Contents

Scott Daniel Ellison	14
Visions on Alligator Alley	15
Parkway Auto Parts	17
Lori Nix	18
Ode to the Wooden Fork that Left a Splinter in Dad's Index Finger	19
Alessandra Sanguinetti	20
Learning about Death	21
Sophie Calle	22
Sunday	23
Onajide Shabaka	24
Chalk Dust	25
Jenny Larsson	26
Summer Solstice	27
Jackie Gendel	28
Ode to the Spork	29
Vera Iliatova	30
I Have My Reasons	31
Marcella Hackbardt	32
Survey of the South Florida Farmlands	33
Natalya Laskis	34
Motor Maintenance	35
My Common Book of Prayer: Poem No. 1	36
Ampersand	37
Sophie Calle	38

The Affair	39
Leandra Arvazzetti	40
Roses	41
Delia Brown	42
Bar Mates	43
Rolling Back the Odometer	44
The Pact	45
Carolyn Swiszcz	46
Sunlight of Florida	47
Aramis Gutierrez	48
Sometimes I Wish My Vagina Had Teeth	49
Melanie Daniel	50
A Flower in the Glade	51
Eye Spy (Flowers on the Alley)	53
Rosemary Laing	54
A Jewish Boy's Guide to Diesel Mechanics	55
Glossary of Automechanics in Four Gears	56
Lisa Sanditz	58
Reflection at 9:38 AM	59
Jenny Larsson	60
Rebirth	61
Penmanship	63
Sanford Biggers	64
Nameless Prayer	65
Christina Pettersson	66
When the Mechanics Go Home	67

Scott Daniel Ellison, "Bog," 2011, Acrylic on Board, 16 x 16" Courtesy the artist.

Visions on Alligator Alley

At this late hour on this August night,
I am again filled with words that aren't chassis nor red
like a roadside flair. Instead, they are eternal,
like time, like matter, as if a second person inside me
is now taking a specific word out
completely from the manifold
and substituting it with intense darkness
scored by vivid red lines.

I see Father alone at times,
body leaned over car with grim determination,
touching hand to the hot big block, like a sheet
to a flame at the bottom of the pile as the fire roars upward.
He smooths his mustache with the back of his hands
as decades of careful work turn black in the cuticles,
mud and grease all around, knuckles full of scars,
his half-witted efforts gin up something good,
something semi-permanent,
like a car crash I can't turn from,
or a vivid memory at the machine shop
interrupted by a moment of weeping
that I too have left behind
so long ago in a shimmering cloud
from the exhaust pipe.

My words are not sad, but bitter,
for all sweetness was cast out the window
on this desolate drive with love for a father.
They flutter in a final breath and then fall
from the sky as an acidic rain.

The shadows on the asphalt
through these Everglades imply my origin,

revealing my lane is really one way.
For so long I've sat idling halfway between
the drainage ditch and the stars.

From my driver's seat
I focus on the grasses.
I focus on the reptiles.
I focus on my father,
a mirage in the passenger seat.

The sun is perched on the horizon in my side view
bursting with the phosphorescence of Independence Day.

No other will tailgate my shadows.
No one else will sleep in my dreams.
This is the emancipating power of nonsense.

Parkway Auto Parts

I remember the machine shop,
your rebuilt transmissions and carburetors,
inventory of fan belt boxes and Quaker State oil,
centerfolds and bikini beer girls,
grease-stained handprints and holes,
and the corner where I stacked Budweiser cans
to make homes and tunnels for my sparkplug people.
The gumball machine outside
the parts room filled with peanut M&M's,
a water cooler by Bill's office door, and how I drank
the summer of '87 over and over from a paper cone cup
just to watch the bubbles fart up to the surface.

That was the year I started kindergarten,
and you called mom a *nothing*,
and she found a job the very next day.

I remember lying next to you one time on the creeper
under a red '67 GTO. You told me that oil was the lifeline
of the vehicle. And I wondered then as I do now
about the harsh words you pushed out the car door when
cheap American brew flowed through your veins.

You've forgotten how many beers you could handle
in an hour, or the handprint you left next to the poster
where you propped yourself after chugging all those cans.
You've forgotten your car passion, or how you could fix anything
except Mom. Although I'm the only girl I know who can change
my own brake pads or set my own rocker arms,
I still don't know what my lifeline is.

Lori Nix, "Living Room," 2013, Archival Pigment Print, 39½ x 66¼" © Lori Nix, Courtesy of ClampArt, New York City.

Ode to the Wooden Fork that Left a Splinter in Dad's Index Finger

I watched my father stab
cheese fries with you,
tongue-depressant shaped,
wooden and flat.
Those were the days
he taught me about
water pumps and gaskets,
how real men were mechanics,
that useful girls can change
their own flat tires curbside.
I remember the chili cheese dogs,
and stack of Caboose slider burgers,
buns soft and soggy, and how he
drank and drank and drank
till I longed to be with
someone not like him.

Alessandra Sanguinetti, "Belinda, Chick and Clock," 2000, Photograph, 9½ x 9" Courtesy the artist.

Learning about Death

It happened because Milton the Manx
crawled into the engine compartment
when I was younger. He was taken
to the Everglades Animal Hospital
to be put down. Not wanting to
keep secrets, Dad explained the dynamics
of the big needle used to kill Milton,
as if the details of euthanasia really mattered
when I was nine. A few weeks later,
Gramm's nurse administered Gramm's insulin shot
one morning at the Sunshine Assisted Living Facility.
By evening, she was gone.

Sophie Calle, "Exquisite Pain (Day 7)," (detail), 2007,
Embroidered text and photograph panels.
Text: 53 x 24⅜", photograph: 19¾ x 24⅜"
Overall dimensions: 75½ x 51½"
© 2015 Sophie Calle / Artists Rights Society (ARS),
New York / ADAGP, Paris. Courtesy of Sophie
Calle and Paula Cooper Gallery, New York.
Photo by Zack Balber, Ginger Photography, Inc, Miami.

It was at home, in Bondy, on May 19, 1980. A Sunday. I was seventeen. We were having a family lunch — my parents, my two brothers and I. At one o'clock, my older brother stood up and said: "There's something I have to do." Before he left he kissed my father. Later, they called my mother on the phone. When she hung up, she used simple-sounding words: "Something happened, Didier, something very serious. I'll be back soon. Don't move." She was crying.

The worst part was between three and five p.m.: two hours waiting for her, two hours on my bed thinking of paralysis, of death, looking through the curtains at the sky. Then, at five p.m., I learned that he had jumped off the train from Bondy to Paris. He was twenty-three. I remember it was a warm, beautiful day. That it was my father's birthday. That we'd all had lunch together. That we had everything we needed for a happy and peaceful Sunday.

Sunday

                        May 19,   A Sunday.
I was seventeen.
                              At one o'clock,

           they called my mother
                  she used simple-sounding
words: "Something happened,   something
    serious. I'll be back

  waiting   two hours on my bed thinking
of paralysis, of death, looking through   curtains at
   sky.   I learned   he had
jumped
         I remember   a warm, beautiful day.
      my father
                              needed
a happy and peaceful Sunday.

Laura McDermott, "Sunday," 2015, Erasure Poem. Digitally altered image based on photograph of "Exquisite Pain (Day 7)" panel by Sophie Calle. See p.22 for original Calle panel.

Onajide Shabaka, "Total Disappearance 1905" (film still), editioned archival print on Canson paper, © 2011 Courtesy the artist.

Chalk Dust

The doctors make me take these white pills,
10 milligrams cut in half.
The jagged edge leaves a chalk line
down the center of my tongue,
as if outlining the corpse of the old me
struck down in the intersection
of two major highways.

This will take the edge off.

It's been two months now,
and each morning they screech down my throat
like nails on the blackboard
or racing slicks on rain-splattered asphalt.

These pills will erase the pain of the past.

I imagine myself back in Miss Washburn's third grade class,
at the blackboard of my brain,
a freshly clapped eraser palmed in my right hand.
In a swirling motion, I wipe it clean,
leaving a pile of white dust on the tray below.
The chalk lines are still faint on the board.
Yet, I can still see my dad throwing back another brewski
with the neighbor mechanics,
cracking jokes outside the front window
about his nine-year-old with C-cups.
And when she's running down
the chalk line of the softball diamond,

she's a bouncing sight to see.

Trying not to breathe,
I force another pill down
in the cloud of clapped erasers,
a shroud of billowing exhaust fumes.

Jenny Larsson, "The Forest Diaries, Part 1: The Film" (still), 2014, Video. Photo: Johan Arthursson/Bjornhult Media.

Summer Solstice

I remember how you looked that long, humid night—rabid and fierce.
Almost three months to the day that Daddy ended it.
Your mother made some kind of bitter holistic root tea we drank.
In the den, your father was practicing Japanese for his next trip,
while your brother Scotty was teaching an egg to do tricks
on the speckled Formica kitchen counter.
We snuck out behind your garage that endless August night
to the vacant parking lot of the Baptist school, to the place where the moon nested
with the mockingbirds in the branches of an old banyan tree.
On the front patio, a one-winged palmetto bug flopped into the wall
as your dog Ankota mercilessly pawed it from one corner to the next.

"Hear that?"
"Hear what?"

As if the music dancing through the leaves gave you reason enough to touch me.

Jackie Gendel, "Book Club," 2009, Oil on canvas, 24 x 22" Image courtesy Girls' Club.

Ode to the Spork

My tongue traces you
through your hollowed-valley navel,
swoops towards your spiky flanked ridge.
I remember the flavors: peaches in heavy syrup,
lumpy tapioca, a hint of bland
plastic, like that of straws.
Your half-moon contour reveals
remnants of my high school life
and memories in parked cars, the eavesdropped
conversations of the lunchroom pinging in my head.
Corn kernels catapulted into my hair and stuck,
like the speedy gossip of my lost virginity.
But you, my versatile tableware, comforted me.
You shoveled in your condolences.

Vera Iliatova, "Practice," 2011, Oil on Canvas, 42 x 36" Courtesy the artist.

I Have My Reasons

Because my father taught me how to change a flat.
Because my mother read Harlequin novels.
Because I watched my sister kiss the neighbor boy on the mouth.
Because I heard her friend say she'd get pregnant if she did.

Because Eldon Pinkerton liked Miriam instead of me.
Because I had C-cups in the fifth grade.
Because everyone talked about it at the lunch table as if they were experts.

Because we dated for thirty-eight months.
Because I was student council president.
Because you were the star football player.
Because we were both amateurs.

Because you ended your letters with "Loving you always and forever."
Because I didn't know how to love myself.
Because you felt it was time.
Because I thought fellatio was a character from *Hamlet*.

Because I had a feeling you'd leave me.
Because it had to happen sooner or later.

Marcella Hackbardt, "Subjectivity," 2008, Digital Chromogenic Print, 21 x 44" Courtesy the artist.

Survey of the South Florida Farmlands
(after Tomas Tranströmer)

A '79 Oldsmobile is planted in a vegetable field. What's it doing this far off-road?
It's a monument to believers in the American dream.
But the migrants have larger visions: hopes of returning to a freer land.
As if this were to happen in their lifetime.

On my way home I see green tomatoes budding
                                        in my porch planter.
They are moons of gravitational pull, radiating a new phase
for those who have sobbed in the darkness of the soil.

Natalya Laskis, "What I Know," 2013, Acrylic and Oil on Canvas, 60 x 48"
Image courtesy Girls' Club.

Motor Maintenance

He is ordinary, a red shop rag
snugly tucked into his Dickie work blues. He is
on the cusp of middle age, appealing in South Florida.
He is a brain surgeon or a sonneteer.
I am in his skin this morning
on a creeper draining the oil pan,
happy to be not too young, happy to be
thrilled that it is warm, and he has grease under his nails.

Everyone is someone other than you think.
The mechanic does not have
liverwurst and onion on white in his brown
bag. He has Godiva and strawberries and a note from his lover half his age,
whom he just left at her condo on the beach before her husband made it home.
When he rolls out from the undercarriage,
and wipes off his strap wrench, our eyes meet.
We smile. Inside, our private, gorgeous lives.

My Common Book of Prayer: Poem No. 1
(for W.)

I've prayed prayers that lingered over your name,
the delicate assembly of vowels and consonants.
I've cradled them. There are no words for this.
Prayers for your peace and salvation. Prayers to draw us closer.
Prayers for you to see with my eyes the man you are
and the man you are becoming. I've nurtured each prayer.
Turned out the lights to let them illuminate the room
with the fire of interstellar dust. Held them to
my chest and wondered what mythic beach
the sand in our hourglass comes from.

What we use every day to open envelopes is something much nobler,
the curve of your cheek bone, explosive ideas, exact use of cologne.
At night, I put my ear to your ear and
listen to the echo of your dreams while I pray.
I pet your collar bone. *What are you thinking?*
I whisper in a language of touch in a dialect unique to us.
I watch the sheets rise gently, hoping the slant of light
will make you turn over.

It's always then our long highways slide out of my hands.
Maybe it's the fault of our language, but my prayers are
innocent and pictorial. My prayers speak for us side by side, leg over leg,
puzzle-pieced, and you, sound asleep,
finger my prayers like braille.

You asked me once why I've never written poems for you,
and I said it's because you never pissed me off enough.
But the truth of the matter is
I've been too busy writing prayers for you.

Ampersand

& we are the symbol
which by itself is
& per se &
regarded as the forgotten 27th letter
rooted in antiquity & a ligature
in the everyday script & fragments
& as a logogrammatic representation of
the conjunction & shaped
figure-8-like or a reversed double-bowled g
we indicate a closer collaboration
& coupling until we break the infinity &
part ways on the side

Sophie Calle, "Exquisite Pain (Day 7)," (detail), 2007, Embroidered text and photograph panels.
Text: 53 x 24⅜", photograph: 19¾ x 24⅜"
Overall dimensions: 75½ x 51½"
© 2015 Sophie Calle / Artists Rights Society (ARS), New York / ADAGP, Paris. Courtesy of Sophie Calle and Paula Cooper Gallery, New York.
Photo by Zack Balber, Ginger Photography, Inc, Miami.

Seven days ago, the man I love left me.
He was a friend of my father's. I had a crush on him even as a little girl, but I was thirty when I seduced him. From time to time he would remind me that he wasn't really in love but I blithely ignored the warning: he was living with me, after all. Then I was offered a study grant for Japan. He threatened to break off the relationship during my three-month absence: it was too long. I decided to go anyway, fearing that otherwise I'd always blame him for the missed opportunity. To comfort me, in spite of his ultimatum, he suggested we meet up in New Delhi, at the end of my journey. I left Paris on October 25, 1984. I hated that trip. Then I got a letter from him. It said, simply: "Darling little wife." He was waiting. And so all I lived for was January 24, the date of our reunion. That day, three hours before his plane took off, he confirmed that he was coming. But at the airport there was a telegram for me: he had had an accident, he was in hospital. I spent part of the night trying to contact him, imagining the worst. It was two in the morning when he picked up the phone. Yes, he had been in hospital, to have an infected finger treated, he said. I knew. A few words blurted out over the phone told me that he had just met another woman, that he hoped it was serious. Before hanging up, I said, "Poor me." I spent the rest of the night in room 261 at the Imperial Hotel, staring at the moldy carpet, the red telephone. India had been his idea. He had made the reservations, chosen this place which would be the setting for my suffering.

The Affair

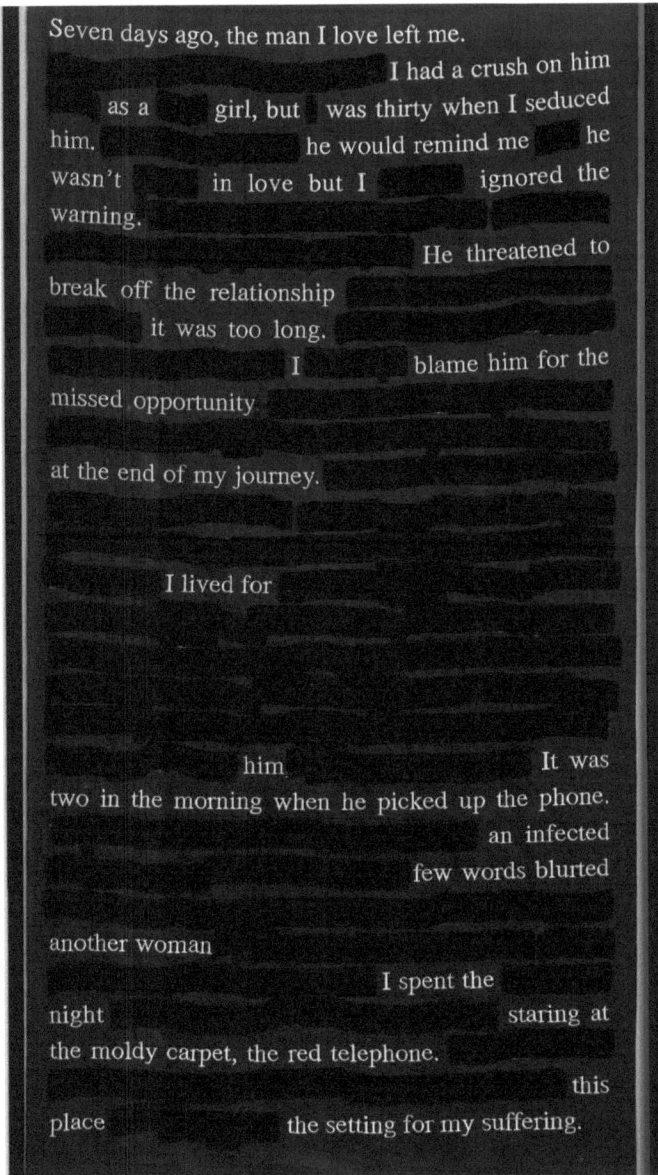

Laura McDermott, "The Affair," 2015, Erasure Poem. Digitally altered image based on photograph of "Exquisite Pain (Day 7)" panel by Sophie Calle. See p.38 for original Calle panel.

Leandra Arvazzetti, "Untitled," 2013, Ceramic, 16 x 10 x 10" Image courtesy Girls' Club.

Roses

Since Valentine's they've rooted here,
dead-blood and dried,
withered over my dining room table,
slumped in murky water,

half-evaporated.
They fill my home with the
pungent aroma of death.
Suffocated baby's breath,
forever-browned greens.

Fringed rugs on cold ceramic tile
and these desiccated twigs of emotions,
like good intentions or peck

kisses,
dry and hard-lipped.
My flop-eared

rabbit toys
with the fallen petals
as if they were injured mice
scattered about the glass tabletop.
She bites,

then sits
back,
and waits for them
to react to
her deliberate advances.

Delia Brown, "Getting Hung Up at a Collector's House en route to the Museum (Katie Watching Leisa Play Bartender)," 2003, Graphite and Gouache on Paper, 10 x 15½" Photo by Gerhard Heidersberger.

Bar Mates

At a quarter past one, the nut shells give
the midtown saloon a grainy feel.
A fly zigzags a defined line
through the thick carbon monoxide air,
and I stew in enough steam to press a dozen shirts.
From the antique cigarette sign overhead,
the Marlboro Man tips his hat in approval,
as if prompting me to call him. Once I've finished
my drink and motioned for another,
the drone in the earpiece wipes out all unfamiliarity.
The people we once loved are now eulogized
by infected cell phone lines and dropped calls.
In Florida he was a mechanic and a surfer boy,
but up in Asheville,
in the hillbilly, foothilled neighborhoods,
he's a landlocked merman with bleach-tipped hair.
If only I could bring myself to say it
—everything before "I love you" doesn't count.
But instead, I press cancel
in fear of speaking Drunkenese.
Licking my salted palm, I can see I was wrong:
Mr. Marlboro wasn't consenting, but rather, shielding his own,
for he too once loved in El Paso,
or was it San Antonio?
but is destined to ride alone forever.
I leave the saloon
broke and confused and don't know why
the sun punches the evening's timecard.

Rolling Back the Odometer

I ran across your old best friend on Facebook
the other day, and he told me the reason
you stopped calling me was because you've got a real girl now.
Eight years ago we began inserting mind games in place of love, yet
I hoped you would break down and say it—or maybe I just wished that I did.
It's too bad our idea of courtship was talking cars or fucking
on the hood of them whenever I was in town, anything I could do
to get you to roll out from under the big block
on the creeper to pay me some attention. But you worked
within the confines of your character, cast
as the bad boy in my life, even your greased cuticles
were right. We don't have a past so much
as a receding row of phone lines and liquor, a connection never fully soldered.
What we had together sounds like a rash, as if we caught
one another, and desire was merely a symptom that could be treated
with the lubricant of late night drunken calls. Thinking of you now,
everything's a blurred scene in my rearview,
but I'm not immune to the memories we made. I still haven't found
an antibody to protect me from the pathogen of your distant voice.
I don't know how long I've lacked a word for "sins of emission."
I don't know how many miles there are between you and me,
but I suspect many more now, or why these burnt-out headlights
travel farther than the incandescent high beams
we switched on so long ago. I'm sorry all the kisses
I keyed across your chest were written
in grease pen. Sometimes I think of you
so hard your old Sonoma drives right out of my pillow
and wakes me, engine revving to let me know
you've come by. I'm sorry this poem never met you.
Instead of wishing that the other would've hopped into the driver's seat,
we should've jumped into the back, both enjoying the ride,
and together tapping out the heartbeat through our exhaust—
all we should have said roaring out the pipes.

The Pact

> "If you ain't first, you're last."
> —Ricky Bobby, *Talladega Nights*

I made a pact with you, mechanic men—
I have detested you long enough.
I come to you as a grown woman
Who had a gear-head father;
I am old enough now to check my own gauges.
It was you who bore the block for the pistons.
We have tie rods and drive shafts between us.
Now is the time for racing.

Carolyn Swiszcz, "Diary, 2001," 2002, Mixed Media on Paper, 15 x 48" Courtesy the artist.

Sunlight of Florida

She does so much damage
with the sway of her hips
as she tap dances on the sand in argyle socks.
The electrodes she's implanted
with her smile and coconut scent,
wait for the wave to break.
He runs fingers up her spine,
her Coppertone tan shimmers in low light,
granules of sand shape her calves.
She is the improvised explosive device
his brain didn't count on,
seeing it was located in his swim trunks.

This beach town is a bit like the memory,
a stained glass summer when the sun
broke free of the squat horizon,
burned off pixel and photon,
simmered mid-sky to heat the air,
made the sperm-like kite
wind like a Möbius strip to
flash and rise over heads of swimmers,
and then plunged into the deep waters of neuroscience.

And the sun
grows small as a period,
as if it couldn't be placed one day
at the end of the charge.

    The moment.
        The backdrop.
            The persona.

Aramis Gutierrez, "The Brief Return of the Megalodon," 2007, Oil on Canvas, 84 x 72"
Courtesy the artist.

Sometimes I Wish My Vagina Had Teeth

I announced after I guzzle down my fifth
Bud late Tuesday night. A vagina-mouth filled
with rows of razor incisors like a thirsty great white.
You'd hear rumbles from my crotch like a twelfth century
dungeon as I crossed my legs. Like the Venus flytrap, I
would lure men into my little shop of horrors with
my delicate petals and sweet aroma. I would
part my thighs, caress my breasts and let out inviting
moans and sighs. After a few thrusts with his lovestick,
my sweet smile would turn down. My *Vaginus Carnivorous*
would clamp onto his dick like a vice, mercilessly
tearing through foreskin. Blood-curdling
screams would be heard from my bedroom,
followed by laughter, screeching. As I fuck,
warm blood and mangled flesh would flow down the remaining shaft,
to his man-berries, and then to the sheets below us. His agony
would bring me great sadistic pleasure. Tormented nights, you'd
see half-dressed men running from my room, bloody,
missing a finger, tongue, penis tip, maybe
a toe or two. People often wonder what
type of a childhood I had. During summer stays
at Grandpa Palumbo's in Pahokee, Florida, I would
sneak to his Polydent-filled cup on the bathroom counter
late at night. Sitting on the cold tile, I'd lower my white cotton
panties just enough to insert his false teeth inside to
practice my pussy grin. A few days ago,
I was watching cosmetic dentistry on the
Discovery Channel. I was really intrigued by the process.
In a couple years, when I can afford it, I'll invest
in my own set of punani porcelains. My father would be proud
at the thought of his little girl having a prochastity mechanism
to protect my virtue. To save the Trojan Warriors
from the clutches of my wicked snatch,
the boys can only hope I develop lockjaw.

Melanie Daniel, "Lotus Eater," 2014, Oil on Canvas, 26 ⅝ x 26 ⅝" Courtesy the artist.

A Flower in the Glade

Barreling through the Everglades on the 85-mile stretch
of two-lane highway linking civilization to civilization
through my abandoned town, a land bridge of asphalt,
you, Lover, appear, bumming a ride.
This flat road stretches like the highway of the mind
leaving garages full of soundless engines,
their echo threading a tunnel, etched with cold moisture
on a solitary wildflower, whose delicate fists
burst in fuchsia without a direction, as gentle signs
emerge from the ashes of a recent burn in the pine.
Their words ashy as they float off into
the afternoon sky of an exasperated summer.

I hold onto the thought that this vehicle of life
could surely carry me to sunnier terrain,
fill my charcoal eyes with laughter once more,
while I drive this path that's taking me onward.

Clutching the steering wheel,
all I have written of you,
flowers in the glade,
opens into bursts of red.
Each honeyed beam
sets these confessional rays,
shackled to my tongue,
loose with the cursive blue of freedom
that makes the wind rise.

But meanings can't be absorbed by your ears — sponges
filled with brackish water needing to be rung out.
Soundless bold wings then carry my words out
the open passenger window.
And as we continually travel on this dream highway,

we are separated by the center console in this vehicle.
We are exiled from the place we began.

My eyes are now the same color as the snakes and gators,
who crawl from grassy ditches to swallow whole the expectations
I placed on my father who tried, despite his drunken faults.

But for you,
they come for blood
dismembering
your head
your body
your heart
and the words
I attempted
to deliver to you.

I pull the Mustang over, leave you
at mile marker 63 in the thicket of this transitional place,
a brush where few leaves are able to hang on.

This is where I evict you as the person inside my struggle,
casting your name towards the heavens to combust in this heat.

Eye Spy (Flowers on the Alley)

Red as a scorned heart,
yet resilient beyond comprehension.

They thrive in manure ground, cracked sidewalks,
filth, mulch, and mud.

Each delicate, a distinctive form—
if only I could capture their essence,

vermilion, sanguine, scarlet—
cockscomb, lobster claw, scorpion orchid, love lies bleeding—

Rosemary Laing, "one dozen unnatural disasters in the Australian landscape #2," 2003, C Type Photograph, 48⅖ x 86½"
© Rosemary Laing, Courtesy Galerie Lelong, New York.

A Jewish Boy's Guide to Diesel Mechanics

Women,
like a Mercedes' engine,
combust when the piston rises,
compresses their mixtures so tight
that they explode with barely a spark.

Glossary of Automechanics in Four Gears

1. *A Childhood Glossary of Automechanics*
accumulator: a child who collects memories to write poems about as an adult
anti-sway bar: a device used to correct dad's drunken stagger
dodge: what mom didn't do well when dad's words hardened
expansion valve: the heart's strategy for pain
mustang: the pony that every little girl wishes for
pickup: used for getting mommy's things from the house
shock absorber: mom
spark plug: a child's toy inside the mechanic's garage
stabilizer bar: a device used to keep dad from falling over when standing
universal joint: a machine shop, a saloon, gallery of nudie posters, day care.

2. *Glossary of a First Love*
accumulator: a young woman who collects kisses to write poems about in later life
anti-sway bar: a stable relationship
dodge: opposite of confront, which is what I chose to do
expansion valve: a dream-capturing device
mustang: she was built like a …
pickup: what we wish men to be
shock absorber: whatever softens the blow of an initial encounter; a pillow or small talk
spark plug: what leads to the next date
stabilizer bar: what is missing at the beginning of a breakup
universal joint: what I kicked him in when I found out

3. Glossary of a Heartbreak
accumulator: a woman who collects hurts to write poems later when she heals
anti-sway bar: a stable person suitable for dating; accountant, football jock, CEO
dodge: a scam
expansion valve: the waistline
mustang: what Prince Charming rode out on
pickup: a sugar high
shock absorber: food and alcohol
spark plug: something to be changed every 30,000 tears or every two years
stabilizer bar: a saloon, ice cream parlor, drinkery, lounge, bakery, pub, tavern,
           patisserie or watering hole
universal joint: therapy

4. Glossary of the Dating Blue Book
accumulator: a woman who writes poems about old lovers in life
anti-sway bar: a monogamous relationship
dodge: a truck with a tow hitch and a nine-foot bed that never needs making
expansion valve: vagina with the insertion of a penis
mustang: my personal pick up line
pickup: any line I fall for
shock absorber: an orgasm
spark plug: one who is sexually promiscuous
stabilizer bar: a man, specifically a mechanic man
universal joint: penis

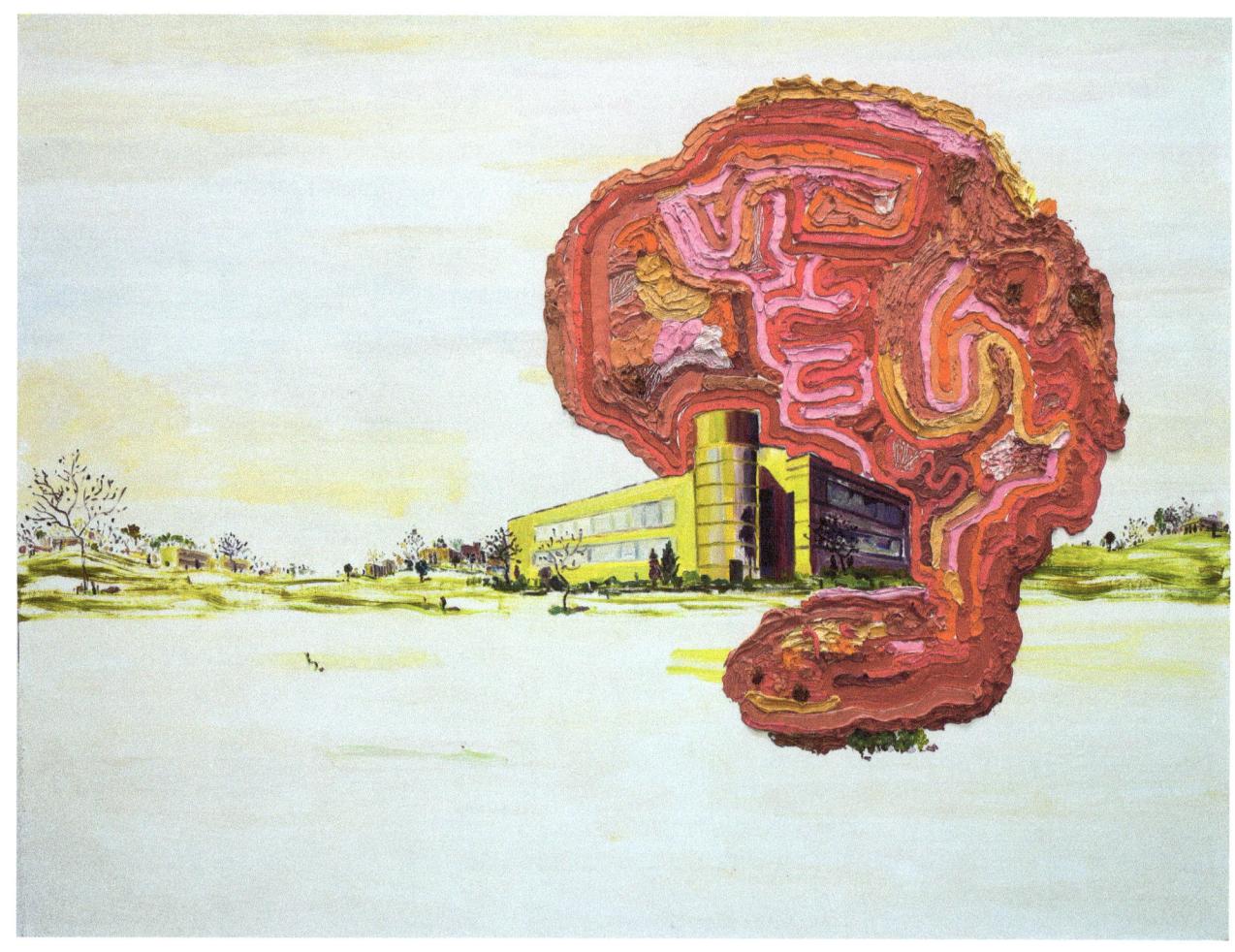
Lisa Sanditz, "Pink Slime," 2012, Mixed Media on Canvas, 30 x 40" Image courtesy Girls' Club.

Reflection at 9:38 AM

The clouds this morning
take three long steps forward
then slink back a half step—
teasing, taunting me

the way only the sun can
when it's missing from the skyscape—
a temperamental gray
like peering into a well.

The inhale to all these exhales,
might catch a glimpse of my reflection
in the scatter of twinkling pinholes poked
through the smog's cloak.

Together, we cover all distance
as we begin to make sense of these moments.
Pulling them out of our pockets like pebbles,
we toss them around to see if they still hurt.

Maybe this is my strength in the darkness,
like peeling back an onion to expose the pink of raw flesh.

I tell you a story my father once shared,
something about how tears are places
for the light to shine through.

Jenny Larsson, "The Forest Diaries, Part 1: The Film" (still), 2014, Video. Photo: Johan Arthursson/Bjornhult Media.

Rebirth

"She moves, and I adore: / Motion can do no more."
—Theodore Roethke

The cliffs rise before her
into summer sky.
She looks at the clear water
in front of her,
surface not appearing to move.
She kneels in the wet moss,
a hush fills the lower valley
with the sound of voices,
the fiery echo of the gods.

A week after solstice,
the trades blow
in the mouth of the valley,
where the sun seems white
glitters on the leaves
and across the blank ponds.
Water runs over rocks,
the frayed clouds
slip behind white crags
with tropical birds who
wheel around them
thousands of feet above.
This is the beginning
where almost anything can end.

Here,
the aria rises to a pitch,
a song of betrayal, salted with revenge.
This is where you find the creation of light.
A fish wriggles onto land,
the rivers lose their names in an ocean.

And the climbing party is stuck on a ledge
halfway up the mountain.
They hang on,
slide down rock by rock
to where a stream flows in from the other side,
the destination we cannot help imagine,
a streak of light burns in the sky.

She puts her mouth to the cold pane
drinks from it with her eyes
plunges her head
and hands into the current.

Everything appears
to be white against the white sky.
It falls upward behind her
until the fires sink
and the voices slow

                      as a whisper.
                              It drifts softly by her cheek.

Penmanship

In my father's hand, I was small capital letters:
An Allen wrench or hex key turned eastward.
A compass set to 32 degrees.
An open pair of needle-nosed pliers.
A dull-headed hammer.
A squared ruler standing on its end.

In my love letters to you,
I was hearts over I's,
Smiley-faces in O's,
your last name added to my first.

On our marriage certificate,
I was the cursive flow of a water fall,
pooled in valleys
garlanded by hillside flax.

On our divorce papers,
I was clean-lined Arial and Times New Roman,
the sterile black and white of a headline.

On my own,
I long to be herbs in a jar,
uncurl my fragrant fingers
rejoice in my frailty and ripeness.

Sanford Biggers, "Quilt #15 Buddha Bless," 2013, Repurposed Quilt, Fabric Treated Acrylic, Spray Paint and Silkscreen, 89 x 70" Courtesy David Castillo Gallery.

Nameless Prayer

Before sleep tonight,
I watch my name dance
in the phosphorescent distance.
Palm fronds drift with the ocean sand,
float around my head,
spawn a voyage
as I drift into twilight,
I feel the beat thumping
beneath the floorboards of my sternum.
My loved ones have moments of uneasiness,
as though they find themselves alone
for the first time in a foreign country. To me,
the faces will be strange and unto themselves,
like birds nested in towers.
I, too, will be high among them,
in a world where I feel alone and of myself.
My forgetfulness will not die in vain.
During my last days of existence,
laughter will replace my withered body
and feeble mind. I will be nothing more
than a memory once my own has left me far behind.

I'm the mumbling in the woodshed,
a prayer without name.

Christina Pettersson, from "my dear leona" series: (clockwise from top left) "Home after 10." "Fr came back." "woods." "El & Rita & I to Canada." 2004–2008, Graphite on Paper, 18 ⅝ x 18 ⅝" Courtesy the artist.

When the Mechanics Go Home

At dusk,
how still
is the shop,
except for roosters
scratching at dust.
The air compressor,
wheel balancer
and impact guns
are caged away,
whistle and tick-free.
The cars
quiet,
their engines
silent
as pendulumless clocks,
timeless.
The Falcon's timing
advanced, energy
stored under the hood,
ready for flight
like soaring birds,
motionless,
yet in motion.

Still,
the time clock
keeps track of these
stagnant moments
until the engines resume
at the crow.

Acknowledgements

my gearhead father who left me with such vividly horrible memories that shaped my poetry, although he barely has a memory of his own now. lard. yellow dye #5. little debbie swiss cake rolls®. four years at zion lutheran high school. walter. being forced to memorize every exit off I-95 between here and miami. many hours wasted on facebook. the fellow writers who aided and abetted my progress, especially mj fievre, jan becker, charlotte howard, katie bennett, as well as my professors and the entire mfa department and alumni of florida international university. bikini season. reality tv shows. the death of mr rogers. mom. ben & jerry's fish food ice cream®. my cat hazel. rainy days. flat tires. sarah michelle rupert and michelle weinberg who gave me this opportunity through girls' club. fisher of pens. dad's alcoholism. guilt. the guy I married who is nothing like my father. dear lord baby jesus. anti-freeze. dunkin' donuts keurig k-cups. spending my childhood in an auto parts store. all beef kosher hot dogs. my sister chrissy and all our shared memories. that old man who fired me because he thought mothers don't belong in poetry. karma. chicken fried steak. my dog farley. bad genes. the green couch. art. #oiaf. family get-togethers. slurpees®. realizing that i'm no longer 16 year after year. brake fluid. silly high school romances and the rebound guys. my colleagues and students of broward college. whole milk. nieces and nephews. the artists who shared their art for this book. the artist formerly known as prince. my fifteen-month-old who bangs on the office door as a plea to come play with her when i've been trapped in my office for too long writing. traffic on the 836. mom, again. chocolate. my in-laws who politely smile and nod when i talk about poetry. flip-flops. morning sickness. my ability to read my cat's mind. my daughter's babysitters tia juana and nanny adele. feminists. talk shows. all the friends, loved ones and strangers who unknowingly donated their own lives to become poems as part of this project.

www.ingramcontent.com/pod-product-compliance
Lightning Source LLC
Chambersburg PA
CBHW042028150426
43198CB00003B/102